DAILY EVENING DEVOTIONAL FOR PRETEEN BOYS AGED 10-12

5-MINUTE DEVOTIONS TO END YOUR DAY WITH REFLECTION, BIBLE LESSONS, AND GOD

BIBLICAL TEACHINGS

Copyright © 2023 by Biblical Teachings -All rights reserved.

No part of this book may be reproduced in any form or by any electronic or mechanical means, including information storage and retrieval systems, without written permission from the author, except for the use of brief quotations in a book review.

Under no circumstances will any blame or legal responsibility be held against the publisher, or author, for any damages, reparation, or monetary loss due to the information contained within this book, either directly or indirectly.

Legal Notice:

This book is copyright protected. It is only for personal use. You cannot amend, distribute, sell, use, quote, or paraphrase any part, or the content within this book, without the author or publisher's permission.

Disclaimer Notice:

Please note that the information contained within this document is for educational and entertainment purposes only. All effort has been executed to present accurate, up-to-date, reliable, complete information. No warranties of any kind are declared or implied. Readers acknowledge that the author is not rendering legal, financial, medical, or professional advice. The content within this book has been derived from various sources. Please consult a licensed professional before attempting any techniques outlined in this book.

By reading this document, the reader agrees that under no circumstances is the author responsible for any losses, direct or indirect, that are incurred due to the use of the information in this document, including, but not limited to, errors, omissions, or inaccuracies.

CONTENTS

Your Journey Begins Here...   vii

1. God's Roadmap   1
2. God's Perfect Timing   3
3. When Things Don't Go As Planned   5
4. From Fear to Faith   7
5. The Power of Prayer   9
6. David and Goliath   12
7. Noah's Ark   13
8. Jonah and the Whale   15
9. Daniel in the Lions' Den   17
10. The Fiery Furnace   19
11. Counting Blessings   22
12. Gratitude in Challenges   24
13. Acts of Kindness   26
14. Grateful for Forgiveness   28
15. Contentment and Gratitude   30
16. Turning Water into Wine   34
17. Healing People in Need   36
18. Feeding the Five Thousand   38
19. Walking on Water   40
20. Calming the Storm   42
21. Understanding Bullying   46
22. Being an Upstander   48
23. Kindness and Empathy   50
24. Inclusion and Acceptance   52
25. Cyberbullying   54
26. Samson's Strength   58
27. Caleb's Courage   60
28. Jonathan's Loyalty   62
29. Joshua's Leadership   64
30. King David's Brave Heart   66

31. Active Playtime	70
32. Healthy Eating	72
33. Calm Breathing	74
34. Tech Breaks	76
35. Sleepy Time Routine	78
36. The Patient Turtle	82
37. The Crafty Snake	84
38. The Faithful Dog	86
39. The Talking Donkey	88
40. The Diligent Ant	90
41. The Beauty of Creation	94
42. God's Masterpiece	96
43. Caring for Creation	98
44. The Miracle of Life	100
45. Finding God in Nature	102
46. The Wisdom of King Solomon	106
47. King Josiah's Faithfulness	108
48. King Saul's Obedience	110
49. The Leadership of King Cyrus	112
50. The Perseverance of King Asa	114
51. The Race of Faith	118
52. Building a Strong Foundation	120
53. Peter - From Failure to Success	122
54. Overcoming Challenges at School	125
55. Sportsmanship and Perseverance	127
56. Dream Big	130
57. Goal-Setting 101	132
58. Learning from Role Models	134
59. Building Skills and Knowledge	136
60. Adapting and Adjusting	138
The End?	141

BIBLE STUDY
-Starter Kit-

Discover a **Simple**, **Powerful** Way to Study **The Bible**

- *No More Guesswork* - Learn to Explore the Bible **with Confidence** and Clarity.

- Discover a Study Method That *Fits Seamlessly into Your Busy Life* - **Without the Overwhelm**.

- **Build a Bible Study Routine** *You'll Actually Look Forward To* - Not Just Another Task on Your To-Do List.

SCAN THE QR CODE FOR YOUR FREE COPY

YOUR JOURNEY BEGINS HERE...

Hey there! Welcome to the second part of this super cool preteen boy devotional series. This book is here to help you handle the good stuff, the tough stuff, and everything in between. Each night, you'll get a chance to chill, think, and hang out with God. Let's get started!

Why This Devotional?

Life can feel pretty crazy, right? There's school, friends, sports, games—it's a lot. This devotional is like a daily pit stop to recharge and remind you that God's got your back. Use it to unwind, get some wisdom, and end your day on a high note.

What's Inside?

- **A Bible Verse:** Start with a quick power-up from God's Word.

- **A Story or Lesson:** These short reads are all about real-life stuff you deal with—making choices, dealing with friends, and growing in your faith.
- **Reflection Questions:** Think about how the story connects to your own life.
- **A Prayer:** Wrap it up by talking to God. Easy, right?

How to Use This Devotional

1. **Find Your Spot:** Pick a chill place where you won't get distracted—your room, the couch, or even your favorite chair.
2. **Grab Your Stuff:** You just need this book, a Bible (if you've got one), and maybe a notebook if you want to write anything down.
3. **Say a Quick Prayer:** Ask God to help you learn something cool and useful.
4. **Date the Devotion:** Write the date at the top of the page. This helps you track your journey and see how God is working in your life over time.
5. **Read and Reflect:** Carefully read the verse & insight. Then take your time to answer the reflection questions. This is where the *real* learning happens!
6. **Talk to God:** Finish by saying the prayer in the book or making up your own. God loves hearing from you!
7. **Stick With It:** Try to do this every night. It's like building a daily habit of hanging out with God.

And hey, before you start, remember this: you are loved, valued, and capable of amazing things. These devotions are here to strengthen your bond with God, help you make solid choices, and inspire you to be a bright light in the world.

YOUR JOURNEY BEGINS HERE...

So grab your book and let's get started on this adventure together. You're going to love where it takes you!

P.S. All scripture quotations are taken from the Holy Bible, New International Version (NIV), unless otherwise noted.

PART 1

TRUSTING GOD'S PLAN

1
GOD'S ROADMAP

___ / ___ / _____

"Trust in the Lord with all your heart and lean not on your own understanding; in all your ways submit to Him, and He will make your paths straight."

— PROVERBS 3:5-6

*D*id you know God has an epic plan for your life? We're talking better than any treasure map or secret mission! He's got a roadmap just for YOU. But sometimes, it's easy to feel lost, like you've taken a wrong turn or you're stuck at a dead end. Maybe you've wondered, *"How am I supposed to figure out the right thing to do?"*

Here's the awesome news: God's not just watching from above, waiting to see if you'll figure it out. He's right there, guiding you step by step! All He asks is that you trust Him and follow His lead. It's kind of like playing a video game where you've got the best cheat code—God knows every move you need to make to reach the best outcome.

When you trust God with your whole heart, it's like handing Him the wheel of a race car. He promises to steer you in the right direction, even when the track gets bumpy. Instead of relying only on what you can see or understand, you can lean on Him—He never gets lost or confused. Pretty incredible, right?

Reflection

Think about a time when you had a big decision to make. Did you ask God for help? How did it go?

Maybe it worked out great, or maybe it didn't go as planned, but you learned something cool along the way.

How could you keep asking God for guidance in the choices you make every day?

Let's Pray

Dear God, thank You for creating a special plan for my life. Sometimes I try to figure everything out on my own, and it gets messy. Help me to trust You with my whole heart and listen to Your guidance. Show me the path You've created for me, and give me the courage to follow it. Amen.

2
GOD'S PERFECT TIMING

___ / ___ / _____

"There is a time for everything, and a season for every activity under the heavens."

— ECCLESIASTES 3:1

*H*ave you ever felt like you're stuck waiting forever for something you really want? Maybe it's a new video game, summer vacation, or even your birthday! Waiting is tough, isn't it? But here's the thing: God's timing is always spot on. He has a perfect schedule for everything in your life—even if it doesn't always match what you want.

Think about the seasons. There's a time for warm, sunny days, a time for colorful autumn leaves, and even a time for snowball fights in winter. Each season has its own purpose, and life is kind of like that too. Sometimes you're in a season of learning, like practicing for a big game or studying for a test. Other times, you're in a season of fun and celebration.

The key is trusting that God knows exactly what you need at the right time. When we feel impatient, it's like planting a seed and expecting it to grow into a tree the next day. That doesn't happen, right? The seed needs time to grow roots, soak up water, and get sunlight. God is doing the same thing in your life—He's growing something amazing, and it'll show up at just the right moment.

So, next time you feel frustrated because something isn't happening as fast as you want, remember that God sees the bigger picture. He knows when the timing is just right for your good.

Reflection

Think about a time when you had to wait for something you really wanted. How did it feel? Did you trust that things would work out, or was it hard to be patient?

What can you learn from that experience about trusting God's timing in the future?

Let's Pray

Dear God, thank You for always knowing what's best for me. Sometimes it's hard to be patient when things don't happen the way I want or as quickly as I hope. Please help me trust Your perfect timing and believe that You are working everything out for good. Teach me to wait with a hopeful and grateful heart. Amen.

3
WHEN THINGS DON'T GO AS PLANNED

___ / ___ / _____

> "In their hearts, humans plan their course, but the Lord establishes their steps."
>
> — PROVERBS 16:9

Life doesn't always go the way we plan, does it? Sometimes, no matter how much we prepare or hope, things can take a sudden turn we didn't expect. Maybe you had a big game or an exciting outing planned, but then it got canceled. Or maybe you studied super hard for a test and didn't get the grade you wanted. It can be frustrating and disappointing, and you might even wonder, *"Why did this have to happen?"*

But here's something incredible: even when things don't go the way we planned, God is still in control. He sees the whole picture—the parts we don't understand yet—and He knows what's best for us. It's like planning a puzzle. Sometimes, the pieces don't fit where we think they should, but when we step back, we realize God's creating a masterpiece.

Sometimes, God allows unexpected things to happen because He's guiding us to something even better. It's not always easy to trust Him in those moments, but when we do, we find peace knowing He's got it all figured out. His plans aren't just good—they're perfect. When we give our plans to God, we can trust Him to guide us, even when life takes an unexpected detour.

Reflection

Think about a time when something didn't go as you planned. How did you feel?

Were you able to trust that God was still in control, or was it hard to understand why things didn't work out?

How can you remind yourself to trust Him the next time life doesn't go as expected?

Let's Pray

Dear God, sometimes I feel disappointed when my plans don't work out the way I want. Please help me to trust You, even when life feels confusing or frustrating. Thank You for guiding my steps and turning unexpected moments into blessings. Teach me to follow Your plan, knowing it's always for my good. Amen.

4
FROM FEAR TO FAITH

___ / ___ / _____

"When I am afraid, I put my trust in you."

— PSALM 56:3

We all get scared sometimes, don't we? Whether it's speaking up in class, hearing a strange noise at night, or facing something really tough, fear can feel overwhelming. But did you know that God is bigger than anything you're afraid of? He's always there to help you through it.

Think of fear like a storm. When it's stormy outside, the wind and rain can seem scary, but you know the storm won't last forever. God is like the safe shelter you can run to. When you're afraid, you can talk to Him, and He'll remind you that you're never alone.

Trusting God doesn't mean your fear will vanish instantly, but it does mean you don't have to face it by yourself. You can ask Him for strength, courage, and peace. Little by little, you'll start to feel braver, knowing He's right there with you. God promises to be your protector, so no matter how big your fear feels, His love is always bigger.

Reflection

What's something that makes you feel afraid?

How can trusting God help you feel braver in those moments?

Take some time to think about how God has been with you before when you were scared. How can that help you trust Him now?

Let's Pray

Dear God, thank You for being with me when I'm afraid. Sometimes fear feels so big, but I know You are bigger. Please fill my heart with courage and peace, and remind me to trust You whenever I feel scared. Thank You for protecting me and helping me move from fear to faith. Amen.

5
THE POWER OF PRAYER

___ / ___ / _____

> *"Then you will call on me and come and pray to me, and I will listen to you."*
>
> — JEREMIAH 29:12

Prayer is an incredible gift that God has given us. Have you ever stopped to think about how amazing it is that you can talk to the Creator of the universe anytime, anywhere? When you pray, you're not just saying words—you're having a conversation with God, and He's listening to you. That's right! The God who made the stars and galaxies wants to hear what's on your heart.

But prayer isn't just about asking God for things, like help on a test or to win your next game. It's also a way to share your joys, worries, and thankfulness with Him. Imagine having a best friend you could tell anything to—God is that and so much more! He cares about every little thing in your life, and when you talk to Him, He promises to listen.

Sometimes, we might feel like God isn't answering our prayers fast enough, or maybe His answer isn't what we expected. But here's the thing: God always answers in the way that's best for us. It might not be right away, and it might not be exactly what we asked for, but we can trust that He knows what we truly need. Prayer isn't just about changing our situation—it's about changing our hearts to trust in God's plan.

When you make prayer a regular part of your day, you'll start to notice something amazing. You'll feel closer to God, like you're walking through life with Him right by your side. And guess what? That's exactly what He wants—for you to draw closer to Him, one prayer at a time.

Reflection

Think about a time when you prayed about something important to you. Did you feel like God was listening? What happened afterward?

How can you use prayer to trust God more and grow closer to Him in your daily life? Take a moment to thank Him for always being there to listen.

Let's Pray

Dear God, thank You for the gift of prayer and for always listening. Help me trust Your plan, even when I don't understand. Teach me to come to You with gratitude, joy, and all my worries. Thank You for always being there. Amen.

PART 2

EPIC BIBLE STORIES

6
DAVID AND GOLIATH

___ / ___ / _____

"The Lord is my strength and my shield; my heart trusts in him, and he helps me. My heart leaps for joy, and with my song I praise him."

— PSALM 28:7

Hey there, mighty warrior! Imagine standing in front of a huge giant, way taller than anyone you've ever seen, with a voice that could shake the ground. That's exactly what David, a young shepherd boy, faced when he stood before Goliath. But here's the incredible part: David didn't have armor, a sword, or even size on his side. So, what did he have? Faith in God.

David knew something super important — his strength didn't come from himself or his weapons. It came from God. With just a sling and a stone, but a whole lot of trust in God, David took down the giant that had everyone else shaking in fear. Amazing, right?

Life can feel a bit like facing Goliath sometimes. Maybe it's a tough test at school, a problem with a friend, or something else that feels way too big to handle. But here's the cool thing: you don't have to face it alone. God is your shield and strength, just like He was for David. When you put your trust in Him, He helps you tackle even the scariest challenges.

So next time you feel small or unsure, remember this: you have the God who helped David on your side. With His strength, there's no challenge too big, no obstacle too tough. You've got this!

Reflection

Think about a time when you faced a challenge that seemed impossible to overcome. How did you find the courage to face it? Did you trust in God's strength?

Reflect on how you can apply the story of David and Goliath to your own life. How can you trust in God's power to help you overcome challenges?

Let's Pray

Dear God, thank You for being my strength and shield. Help me trust in Your power to overcome challenges in my life. Just as You helped David face Goliath, I know You will help me face my own giants. Give me the courage to trust in You and rely on Your strength. Amen.

7
NOAH'S ARK

___ / ___ / _____

"So Noah did everything as God commanded him."

— GENESIS 6:22

*H*ey there, fearless explorer! Have you ever faced a task that felt way too big? Imagine being told to build a massive boat—an ark—and gather two of every kind of animal! That's exactly what God asked Noah to do. Even though it seemed impossible, Noah didn't hesitate. He trusted God and followed His instructions, even when others may have doubted him.

Noah's story teaches us two powerful lessons: obedience and trust. When God warned him about the coming flood, Noah didn't question—he got to work. Day after day, he built the ark, following every detail of God's plan. It wasn't easy, but his faith gave him the strength to keep going.

The ark wasn't just for Noah and his family—it was a safe haven for every animal God created. Imagine the sight of lions, elephants, birds, and even tiny insects all boarding the ark. Through this, God showed His deep care for all living things, including you!

Just like Noah, we may face challenges that seem too big to handle. But when we trust God and take the first step, He will guide us every step of the way.

Reflection

Think about a time when you had to follow instructions or obey someone's guidance, even when it felt tough. How did things turn out?

Reflect on how Noah trusted and obeyed God's commands. How can his story encourage you to trust in God's wisdom and plan for your life?

Let's Pray

Dear God, thank You for the amazing story of Noah and the ark. Help me to have the courage to obey Your commands and trust in Your plans, even when they seem challenging. Like Noah, teach me to listen to Your voice and follow Your guidance with faith and patience. Thank You for loving and caring for all Your creations, including me. Amen.

8
JONAH AND THE WHALE

___ / ___ / _____

> "Trust in the Lord with all your heart and lean not on your own understanding; in all your ways submit to him, and he will make your paths straight."
>
> — PROVERBS 3:5-6

*H*ey there, adventurous spirit!

The story of Jonah and the whale is an incredible lesson about trusting and obeying God—even when we don't want to. Jonah was a prophet with a special job from God: to tell the people of Nineveh to stop doing bad things and turn back to Him. But Jonah didn't want to go! He ran the other way, hopping on a ship to escape.

God had other plans. He sent a powerful storm that rocked the boat. The sailors were terrified, but Jonah knew the storm was because he had disobeyed. To save everyone, he told them to throw him into the sea. As Jonah sank, God sent a giant fish to swallow him whole! Inside the fish for three days, Jonah had plenty of time to think—and pray. He realized that running from God wasn't the answer, so he promised to do what God asked.

The moment Jonah obeyed, everything changed. The fish spat him out onto dry land, and he finally went to Nineveh. To his surprise, the people listened! They turned from their bad ways, and God showed them mercy. Jonah learned an important lesson: God is patient, loving, and always ready to forgive.

Sometimes, we may not understand or even like what God asks us to do. But His plans are always for the best! Instead of running away like Jonah, we can choose to trust God from the start. Who knows? The adventure might be bigger—and better—than we ever imagined!

Reflection

Think about a time when it was hard to obey or trust God's plan. How did things turn out?

Remember Jonah's story. How can you obey God and trust Him more in your life?

Let's Pray

Dear God, I want to follow Your plans. Help me trust and obey You, even when it's hard. Thank You for Your patience and love. Guide me in the right way and help me see that Your plans are best. Amen.

9
DANIEL IN THE LIONS' DEN

___ / ___ / _____

"So do not fear, for I am with you; do not be dismayed, for I am your God. I will strengthen you and help you; I will uphold you with my righteous right hand."

— ISAIAH 41:10

*H*ey there, faithful friend!

The story of Daniel in the lions' den is a powerful reminder that courage and faithfulness can overcome fear. Daniel was a man who loved and followed God, even when it was dangerous. At the time, a law was made that banned praying to anyone except the king. But Daniel didn't let fear stop him—he continued to pray three times a day, knowing it could get him into serious trouble.

Sure enough, the king's jealous advisors caught Daniel and reported him. Because the law couldn't be changed, the king had no choice but to throw Daniel into a den filled with hungry lions. Can you imagine being surrounded by roaring lions, with no way to escape? But Daniel wasn't afraid—he trusted that God was with him. In an incredible act of protection, God sent an angel to shut the lions' mouths, and Daniel stayed safe all night.

The next morning, the king ran to the den, hoping Daniel had survived. When he saw that Daniel was unharmed, he was amazed! He declared that Daniel's God was the true and living God, powerful enough to save and protect His people.

This story teaches us that when we stay faithful, God is always with us. No matter what challenges we face, we're never alone. Just like Daniel, we can trust that God's strength is greater than any fear, and He will help us through life's toughest moments!

Reflection

Think about a time when it was hard to stay faithful to God. How did you feel? Remember Daniel's story.

How can you trust God to protect you and help you stay strong in tough times?

Let's Pray

Dear God, thank You for always protecting me. Help me stay faithful, even when life is hard. Just like You kept Daniel safe, I know You are with me. Give me strength and remind me of Your love when I feel afraid. Amen.

10
THE FIERY FURNACE

___ / ___ / _____

"When you pass through the waters, I will be with you; and when you pass through the rivers, they will not sweep over you. When you walk through the fire, you will not be burned; the flames will not set you ablaze."

— ISAIAH 43:2

*H*ey, fearless believer!

The story of the Fiery Furnace is an incredible lesson about trusting God no matter what. Shadrach, Meshach, and Abednego were ordered to bow to a giant gold statue, but they refused. They stayed faithful to God, even when the king threatened to punish them.

The king was furious and had them thrown into a blazing furnace. But they weren't afraid. They said, *"Our God can save us, but even if He doesn't, we still won't bow down."* That's unshakable faith!

When the king looked into the fire, he was shocked—there weren't just three men inside, but four! God had sent an angel to protect them, and the flames didn't harm them at all—not even their clothes smelled like smoke! The king was so amazed that he praised God, realizing His power was greater than any earthly ruler.

This story reminds us that God is always with us, even in life's toughest moments. When we face our own "fiery furnaces," we can stand strong, knowing that God is by our side, protecting and strengthening us every step of the way.

Reflection

Think about a time when you needed to trust God during a tough situation. How did you respond?

Remember the story of the Fiery Furnace. How can you trust God more in your life?

Let's Pray

Dear God, thank You for always being with me. Help me trust You, even when life is hard. Just like You protected Shadrach, Meshach, and Abednego, I know You will take care of me. Give me courage and help me stand strong in faith. Amen.

PART 3

BEING GRATEFUL

11
COUNTING BLESSINGS

___ / ___ / _____

"Give thanks to the Lord, for he is good; his love endures forever."

— PSALM 107:1

*C*ounting your blessings helps you have a grateful heart. Every day, we are surrounded by blessings, big and small, but sometimes, we're too busy to notice them. When we pause to reflect and appreciate these blessings, it shifts our focus. Instead of dwelling on what we lack, we recognize all that we have. Gratitude changes how we feel, helps us see the good in our lives, and reminds us of God's love and faithfulness.

Think about the warmth of the sun on your face, the laughter of friends, the kindness of a family member, or even the simple gift of a new day. These are not just ordinary moments—they are signs of God's care. Sometimes, we expect blessings to be big and obvious, but many of God's greatest gifts are found in the little things we often take for granted. His love is woven into our daily lives in ways we may not always notice.

Making gratitude a habit doesn't mean ignoring life's challenges—it means choosing to focus on God's goodness even in difficult times. When we count our blessings, our perspective changes. Instead of focusing on what's wrong, we see how God is working in our lives. Gratitude strengthens our faith, brings joy, and helps us trust that God is always providing for us.

Reflection

What are some blessings in your life?

How can you make it a habit to notice them and thank God?

How does being grateful change the way you see the world around you?

Let's Pray

Dear God, thank You for all the blessings You've given me. Help me to notice them and be grateful every day. Teach me to have a heart full of gratitude and to always see Your goodness. Amen.

12
GRATITUDE IN CHALLENGES

___ / ___ / _____

"Give thanks in all circumstances; for this is God's will for you in Christ Jesus."

— 1 THESSALONIANS 5:18

Being grateful can change how we see tough times. It's not always easy to give thanks when things go wrong, but gratitude helps us focus on what's still good. Instead of only seeing the problem, we start noticing how God is helping us through it. Hard times can feel overwhelming, but when we choose to be thankful, we remind ourselves that we are never alone. God is always working, even when we don't understand what's happening.

When we thank God in difficult moments, we invite Him to work in our hearts. Gratitude doesn't mean pretending everything is okay—it means trusting that God is still in control. He can use challenges to help us grow, making us stronger, wiser, and more hopeful. Sometimes, the hardest moments teach us the most important lessons. They help us rely on God more and remind us that He is always with us.

Life won't always be easy, but when we look for the good, we start to notice God's little blessings. A kind word from a friend, a peaceful moment in a busy day, or the strength to keep going —these are all ways God shows us His love and care. When we focus on these blessings, our hearts feel lighter, and we remember that God is always faithful.

Reflection

What's something good that has come from a hard time in your life?

How can you practice being grateful even when things aren't going your way?

What small blessings can you thank God for today?

Let's Pray

Dear God, thank You for being with me in good times and bad. Help me to find reasons to be grateful, even during challenges. Teach me to trust Your plan and see the blessings You give me every day. Amen.

13
ACTS OF KINDNESS

___ / ___ / _____

"Be kind and compassionate to one another, forgiving each other, just as in Christ God forgave you."

— EPHESIANS 4:32

Kindness has the power to make a big difference, no matter how small the act. The verse from Ephesians reminds us to be kind, caring, and forgiving, just as God is kind and forgiving to us. Kindness isn't just about grand gestures—it's found in simple, everyday actions. A smile, a helping hand, or a few encouraging words can brighten someone's day more than we realize.

Think about how it feels when someone is kind to you. Maybe a friend helped you when you were struggling, or someone included you when you felt left out. Those moments of kindness stick with us because they remind us that we are loved and valued. A simple "thank you" can go a long way in letting someone know their kindness mattered.

ACTS OF KINDNESS

Just like we receive kindness, we're called to share it with others. Helping a friend, showing patience, forgiving someone who hurt you, or even choosing to speak kindly instead of reacting in frustration are all ways to reflect God's love. The amazing thing about kindness is that it creates a ripple effect—one small act can inspire others to spread love too.

When we make kindness a habit, we don't just make the world a better place—we become a reflection of God's love to everyone around us. Even in moments when kindness feels difficult, remembering how much kindness and grace God has shown us can give us the strength to do the same.

Reflection

Think about a time when someone was kind to you. How did it make you feel? How can you show gratitude to them?

Reflect on the verse from Ephesians 4:32. How can you be more kind to others and show God's love through your actions?

What is one small act of kindness you can do today to make someone's day a little brighter?

Let's Pray

Dear God, thank You for the kindness You've shown me. Help me to show kindness to others and express gratitude to those who are kind to me. Let my actions reflect Your love and inspire others to do the same. Amen.

14
GRATEFUL FOR FORGIVENESS

___ / ___ / _____

"Bear with each other and forgive one another if any of you has a grievance against someone. Forgive as the Lord forgave you."

— COLOSSIANS 3:13

Forgiveness is one of God's greatest gifts to us. This verse from Colossians reminds us to forgive others, just as God has forgiven us. When we truly accept God's forgiveness, it changes our hearts and helps us extend that same grace to others.

Think about a time when you made a mistake and someone forgave you. How did it feel? Forgiveness lifts a weight off our shoulders, bringing peace and restoring relationships. God's forgiveness not only erases our sins but also teaches us how to let go of anger and hurt. It's not always easy to forgive, especially when we feel wronged, but when we choose forgiveness, we reflect God's love and invite healing into our lives.

GRATEFUL FOR FORGIVENESS

Holding onto resentment can feel like carrying a heavy burden, but forgiveness sets us free. It doesn't mean we ignore the hurt or pretend it didn't happen—it means we trust God to heal our hearts and bring peace. Forgiving doesn't excuse someone's actions, but it allows us to move forward without bitterness.

When we choose to forgive, we honor God and show gratitude for the forgiveness He has given us. God's love is limitless, and He calls us to share that love by extending grace to others. Let's be people who forgive freely, bringing peace, love, and healing to the world around us.

Reflection

Think about a time you were forgiven. How did it change your relationship?

How can you show gratitude for forgiveness?

Is there someone in your life you need to forgive? How can you take a step toward letting go of hurt today?

Let's Pray

Dear God, thank You for forgiving me. Help me to forgive others with the same grace You have shown me. Teach me to have a heart full of gratitude and to show Your love through forgiveness. Amen.

15
CONTENTMENT AND GRATITUDE

___ / ___ / _____

> *"I know what it is to be in need, and I know what it is to have plenty. I have learned the secret of being content in any and every situation, whether well fed or hungry, whether living in plenty or in want."*
>
> — PHILIPPIANS 4:12

In a world that constantly tells us we need more to be happy, learning contentment can be tough. Ads and social media often make us feel like we're missing out. But true contentment isn't about having more—it's about trusting God and appreciating what we already have.

Think about the things you're thankful for right now. It could be something big, like your family, or something small, like a peaceful moment in your day. When we focus on gratitude, we begin to see how much God has already blessed us. Instead of chasing after what we don't have, we learn to appreciate the gifts He has given us.

Gratitude shifts our focus from what's missing to what's present. It fills us with joy and peace, reminding us that God is always providing, even in ways we don't always see. Choosing contentment doesn't mean we stop growing—it means we trust that what God has given us today is enough.

Reflection

What are some areas where you can practice contentment?

How can you thank God for the blessings you already have?

Reflect on the verse from Philippians 4:12 and think about how you can trust God and find joy in all situations.

Let's Pray

Dear God, thank You for the blessings You've given me. Help me to be content and trust You in all situations. Teach me to focus on what I have and not what I lack. May my heart always be full of gratitude. Amen.

PART 4

THE MIRACLES OF JESUS

16
TURNING WATER INTO WINE

___ / ___ / _____

> *"What Jesus did here in Cana of Galilee was the first of the signs through which he revealed his glory; and his disciples believed in him."*
>
> — JOHN 2:11

*J*esus performed His first miracle at a wedding in Cana by turning water into wine. This miracle shows us His incredible ability to bring joy and abundance into our lives.

In John 2:7-9a, Jesus asked the servants to fill jars with water, and He transformed that water into the finest wine. Just as Jesus brought joy and abundance to the wedding, He wants to bring joy and abundance into your life, too. Jesus cares about the details of your life and desires to fill it with His blessings.

This story reminds us that even when things seem ordinary or lacking, Jesus can transform them into something extraordinary. When we invite Him into our lives and trust Him with what we have, He can do more than we ever thought possible. He turns our weaknesses into strengths and brings beauty into situations that seem hopeless.

When we trust Jesus and invite Him into our lives, He can transform ordinary moments into extraordinary ones. Let's open our hearts to His miracles and believe in His power to bring joy and abundance into every aspect of our lives.

Reflection

Consider a situation where you have seen God's provision and experienced His joy. How did it make you feel?

How can you express gratitude for His abundance?

Reflect on the verse from John 2:11. How does it inspire you to trust in Jesus' power to bring joy and abundance?

Let's Pray

Dear Jesus, thank You for Your power to bring joy and abundance into my life. I am grateful for Your provision and the miracles You have worked. Help me to trust in Your power and believe in Your ability to bring blessings and joy. May Your miracles strengthen my faith and bring glory to Your name. Amen.

17
HEALING PEOPLE IN NEED

___ / ___ / _____

"He heals the brokenhearted and binds up their wounds."

— PSALM 147:3

Jesus had immense compassion for those who were suffering. In Matthew 14:14, it says that when Jesus saw a large crowd, He was filled with compassion and healed their sick. This shows His deep care for both physical and emotional needs.

Throughout His ministry, Jesus performed countless healing miracles. Each miracle was an act of love and compassion for those who were hurting. Whether it was restoring sight to the blind, healing the sick, or comforting the brokenhearted, Jesus brought hope, restoration, and transformation to all who encountered Him.

The miracles of Jesus remind us that He is still the same today. His love, compassion, and healing power are available to us no matter what we are going through. He sees our pain and walks with us through it, offering comfort and strength to face each day.

Even today, when we face sickness, pain, or challenges, we can turn to Jesus with faith. He sees our struggles, and His compassion remains available to us. Jesus' healing power can restore not only our bodies but also our hearts and souls. Let's trust in His power to bring wholeness and renewal to every area of our lives.

Reflection

Consider a time when you witnessed or experienced healing, whether physical or emotional. How did it impact your life?

How can you express gratitude for Jesus' healing power?

Reflect on the verse from Psalm 147:3. How does it inspire you to show compassion and care for those who are suffering?

Let's Pray

Dear Jesus, thank You for Your compassion and healing power. I am grateful for the times when You have brought healing to my life or the lives of others. Help me to show compassion and care for those who are suffering. Use me as an instrument of Your healing love. Amen.

18
FEEDING THE FIVE THOUSAND

___ / ___ / _____

> *"Taking the five loaves and the two fish and looking up to heaven, he gave thanks and broke the loaves. Then he gave them to the disciples, and the disciples gave them to the people."*
>
> — MATTHEW 14:19

𝓐nother one of Jesus' most incredible miracles was feeding the five thousand with just five loaves of bread and two fish. In Luke 9:16-17, Jesus took what seemed like a small amount and multiplied it to feed an enormous crowd.

Jesus' miracle of multiplying the loaves and fishes teaches us about His power to provide and His abundant goodness. He turned what was available into more than enough to satisfy everyone's hunger. Through this act, Jesus not only met the people's physical needs but also demonstrated His love and care for them.

This story reminds us that God can use even our smallest offering and turn it into something extraordinary. Whether it's our talents, resources, or time, He multiplies our efforts when we place them in His hands. Jesus shows us that we are never too small or too insignificant for Him to use.

Just as Jesus provided for the crowd, He can provide for us, too. When we offer what we have to Jesus—whether it's our time, talents, or resources—He can multiply it and use it to meet our needs and bless others. Let's trust in His provision and believe that He can do great things when we rely on Him.

Reflection

Think about a time when you witnessed or experienced God's provision in a miraculous way. How did it make you feel?

How can you express gratitude for His abundance?

Reflect on the verse from Matthew 14:19. How does it inspire you to trust in Jesus' provision and recognize His abundant goodness?

Let's Pray

Dear God, thank You for Your provision and abundant goodness. I am grateful for the times when You have provided for my needs in miraculous ways. Help me to trust in Your provision and recognize Your abundance in my life. May I always give thanks for Your provision and share what I have with others. Amen.

19
WALKING ON WATER

___ / ___ / _____

"Take courage! It is I. Don't be afraid."

— MATTHEW 14:27

One of Jesus' incredible miracles was walking on water. In Matthew 14:27, when His disciples saw Him walking on the stormy sea, Jesus reassured them by saying, *"Take courage! It is I. Don't be afraid."*

This miracle shows us that even in the midst of stormy situations, Jesus is with us. He calls us to have courage and not be afraid because He has power over every circumstance. Just as Jesus walked on water, He can help us navigate through the challenges and storms of life.

This story also reminds us that when we fix our eyes on Jesus, we can rise above the storms around us. Like Peter, who stepped out of the boat to walk on the water, we can do incredible things when we have faith and trust in Him. Jesus gives us the courage to face the impossible and the strength to persevere.

When we encounter difficulties, we can find comfort in Jesus' presence. He is always with us, ready to calm our fears and provide guidance. Let's trust Him and have faith, knowing that He can carry us through any stormy situation.

Reflection

Consider a time when you faced a challenging situation and felt Jesus' presence and peace. How did it strengthen your faith?

How can you express gratitude for His comfort in stormy times?

Reflect on the verse from Matthew 14:27. How does it inspire you to trust Jesus and not be afraid in difficult situations?

Let's Pray

Dear Jesus, thank You for Your presence and peace in the midst of storms. I am grateful for the times when You have calmed the storms in my life. Help me to trust You and not be afraid, knowing that You are with me. Strengthen my faith and grant me courage to face any challenges that come my way. Amen.

20
CALMING THE STORM

___ / ___ / _____

"He got up, rebuked the wind, and said to the waves, 'Quiet! Be still!' Then the wind died down and it was completely calm."

— MARK 4:39

Jesus showed His power over nature when He calmed a raging storm. In Mark 4:39, He commanded the wind and waves to be still, and they obeyed Him. This incredible act reveals Jesus' authority over all creation and His ability to bring peace in chaotic moments.

Sometimes life can feel like a big storm with worries and troubles swirling around us. But just as Jesus calmed the storm, He can bring peace to our hearts. When we feel overwhelmed, we can trust that Jesus has the power to calm any storm we face and restore a sense of calm within us.

CALMING THE STORM

This story also reminds us that Jesus is always present, even when it feels like He might be far away. The disciples panicked because they thought Jesus didn't care, but He was right there with them in the boat. Likewise, Jesus is with us through every trial, offering His peace and strength to carry us through.

When we trust Jesus, He not only calms the external storms but also brings peace to our inner struggles. He invites us to lean on Him in times of fear and uncertainty, reminding us that His presence is our refuge. Let's have faith in His ability to bring calm to our lives, no matter what we're going through.

Reflection

Think about a time when you felt worried or afraid, like being in the middle of a storm. How did you find comfort or peace?

How can you trust Jesus to calm the storms in your life?

Reflect on the verse from Mark 4:39. How does it inspire you to seek peace in Jesus' presence?

Let's Pray

Dear Jesus, thank You for Your power to calm the storms of life. When I feel worried or afraid, help me to trust in Your presence and find peace. Please calm the storms in my life and grant me the courage to face any challenges. Amen.

PART 5

STOPPING BULLIES

21
UNDERSTANDING BULLYING

___ / ___ / _____

"Do not repay evil with evil or insult with insult. On the contrary, repay evil with blessing, because to this you were called so that you may inherit a blessing."

— 1 PETER 3:9

*B*ullying is when someone keeps being mean, hurting, or picking on someone else with their words or actions. It can happen in different ways, like hitting, name-calling, or even online. The Bible teaches us that bullying is wrong and can hurt people in ways we might not see. The first step to stopping it is knowing it's not okay.

If you see bullying, remember what God tells us: don't fight back with anger or try to get even. Instead, show kindness and love, even when it's hard. Jesus showed us how to do this. He forgave people and treated everyone with care, even those who were mean to Him.

UNDERSTANDING BULLYING

Standing up to bullying isn't just about talking—it's about doing the right thing. If you see someone being bullied, stand up for them. Be their friend, or let an adult know what's happening. Your support can make a big difference. Showing respect and kindness can help make everyone feel safe and valued.

When you choose to be kind instead of mean, you set an example for others. You show them what it means to follow Jesus by making a positive impact. Let's work together to treat everyone with love and respect, even when it's tough. That way, we can be a light that points to Jesus' love and forgiveness.

Reflection

Think about a time when you saw someone being bullied. How did it make you feel?

What can you do to show kindness and help someone who is being picked on?

Reflect on 1 Peter 3:9. How does it encourage you to stand up against bullying?

Let's Pray

Dear God, thank You for teaching us to be kind and respectful. Help me see when bullying is happening and give me the courage to help. Show me how to stand up for others and make sure everyone feels safe. Let my actions show Your love and kindness. Amen.

22
BEING AN UPSTANDER

___ / ___ / _____

"Speak up for those who cannot speak for themselves, for the rights of all who are destitute."

— PROVERBS 31:8

Standing up for others is one of the most important things you can do. Proverbs 31:8 reminds us that God wants us to speak up for people who can't speak for themselves and to protect those who need help.

If you see someone being bullied, don't stay silent. You can help by being kind to the person being hurt, telling a trusted adult, or calmly standing up to the bully. Your actions can show others what it means to care and make the world a better place.

It's not always easy to be an upstander, but it's the right thing to do. It takes bravery and a big heart to stand up for what's right. When you choose kindness and fairness, you help create a safe and happy place for everyone around you.

BEING AN UPSTANDER

Every time you take a stand, you're showing others how to be kind and brave too. Your actions can inspire others to follow your example and spread kindness. Ask God to give you the strength to always do what's right, even when it's hard.

Reflection

Think about a time when you saw someone being bullied and decided to help. How did it feel to stand up for them?

How can you keep supporting others who need help?

Reflect on the verse from Proverbs 31:8. How does it encourage you to speak up for what's right?

Let's Pray

Dear God, thank You for helping me be brave and kind. Teach me to stand up for others and show kindness to everyone. Help me to speak out when someone needs help and to be a good friend to others. Let my actions make the world a safer and happier place. Amen.

23
KINDNESS AND EMPATHY

___ / ___ / _____

"Be kind and compassionate to one another, forgiving each other, just as in Christ God forgave you."

— EPHESIANS 4:32

Kindness is like a superpower that can change someone's day. When you show kindness to someone, you're sharing a bit of God's love with them. Ephesians 4:32 reminds us to be kind and forgiving, just like God is toward us through Jesus. This verse is a great reminder that kindness and forgiveness go hand in hand.

When you see someone having a tough time, being kind is about more than just saying nice words. It's about stepping into their shoes and understanding what they're going through. That's what empathy means—thinking about how others feel and trying to help. Maybe a friend had a bad day, or someone was left out. You can make them feel better by being there for them.

KINDNESS AND EMPATHY

Did you know small acts of kindness can make a big difference? Even holding the door open, sharing a snack, or saying something encouraging can brighten someone's mood. When we choose to be kind and caring, we create a world where people feel safe and valued. It's like planting seeds of God's love in the hearts of others.

Kindness and empathy don't just help others; they change us too. Every time you choose to care about someone else, you grow closer to being the person God wants you to be. You're showing others what God's love looks like in action. Let's make kindness our habit and choose empathy every day. Remember, even small things can make a huge impact when done with love.

Reflection

Think about a time when someone showed kindness and empathy toward you. How did it make you feel?

How can you show kindness and empathy to others, especially those who might be feeling left out or bullied?

Let's Pray

Dear God, thank You for showing us kindness and compassion. Help me to be kind, understanding, and caring toward others. Show me ways to notice when someone is feeling down and needs a friend. Give me the courage to stand up for kindness and create a world where everyone feels respected and loved. Amen.

24
INCLUSION AND ACCEPTANCE

___ / ___ / _____

> "Just as each of us has one body with many members, and these members do not all have the same function, so in Christ we, though many, form one body, and each member belongs to all the others."
>
> — ROMANS 12:4-5

Inclusion means welcoming and accepting others, appreciating their differences, and recognizing that we are all part of the same community. God created each of us with unique abilities and purposes, and when we come together, we can make something beautiful.

Think about a puzzle. Each piece is different, but every piece is needed to complete the picture. In the same way, each person has a special role in our community. When we embrace and respect these differences, we create a safe and happy space where everyone feels like they belong.

INCLUSION AND ACCEPTANCE

Being inclusive means treating others with kindness and respect, no matter how different they may seem. Maybe someone in your class speaks a different language, has a unique talent, or struggles with something you find easy. Instead of ignoring those differences, celebrate them! Learn from each other, and find ways to connect and grow together.

Let's be the kind of people who bring others together. When we make everyone feel included, we show God's love in action. Together, we can create a community where no one is left out, everyone's voice is heard, and each person feels valued. Remember, true strength comes from unity and acceptance.

Reflection

Think about a time when you felt included and accepted. How did it make you feel?

How can you show kindness and inclusivity toward others who may be different from you?

Let's Pray

Dear God, thank You for creating us all uniquely and reminding us of the value of inclusion. Help me to appreciate and embrace the differences in others, treating everyone with kindness and acceptance. Guide me to contribute to a community where everyone feels welcomed and valued. Amen.

25
CYBERBULLYING

___ / ___ / _____

"Do to others as you would have them do to you."

— LUKE 6:31

In today's digital world, it's important to understand what cyberbullying is and how to prevent it. Cyberbullying happens when someone uses technology—like social media, messaging apps, or gaming platforms—to hurt, embarrass, or threaten another person. But as followers of Jesus, we are called to treat everyone with kindness and respect, both online and offline.

The verse from Luke 6:31, often called the Golden Rule, reminds us to treat others the way we want to be treated. Before posting or commenting online, think about how your words might affect someone. Imagine how it would feel if someone said something hurtful to you. When we choose kind words instead of hurtful ones, we create a safer and more positive space online for everyone.

Being a responsible digital citizen means standing up for others when you see them being mistreated online. If you notice cyberbullying, speak out against it by offering support to the person being targeted or by reporting the harmful behavior to a trusted adult. Your actions can help someone feel valued and safe, even in a tough situation.

Jesus teaches us to love and care for others, no matter where we are—even in the digital world. By being mindful of what we say and do online, we can be a light for others to follow. Let's strive to use technology to spread kindness, encouragement, and God's love to everyone we interact with.

Reflection

Think about how you use technology and social media. How can you promote kindness and respect in your online interactions?

How can you be a positive influence and stand up against cyberbullying?

Let's Pray

Dear God, thank You for the gift of technology and the internet. Help me use it responsibly and treat others with kindness and respect online. Protect me from cyberbullying and guide me to be a positive influence in the digital world. Show me how to support those who may be affected by cyberbullying. Amen.

PART 6

HEROES OF FAITH

26
SAMSON'S STRENGTH

___ / ___ / _____

"Then Samson prayed to the Lord, 'Sovereign Lord, remember me. Please, God, strengthen me just once more, and let me with one blow get revenge on the Philistines for my two eyes.'"

— JUDGES 16:28

The story of Samson teaches us about using the gifts God has given us wisely and following His plan. Samson was blessed with amazing strength, but he didn't always use it in the right way. In Judges 16:28, Samson prayed to God, asking for strength one last time to fulfill God's purpose.

Samson's strength was a gift from God, but he learned the hard way that it's important to use our gifts responsibly. He made mistakes and faced consequences, but in the end, he turned back to God and asked for help. This shows us that no matter how many mistakes we've made, we can always ask God for forgiveness and guidance.

Just like Samson, you have special gifts and talents. Maybe you're good at sports, helping others, or making people laugh. Whatever your gifts are, God gave them to you for a reason. He wants you to use them to make a difference and show His love to others. It's important to use what you've been given in ways that honor Him and help others.

When we surrender our gifts to God and trust Him to guide us, He can do amazing things through us. God's plan is always bigger and better than anything we can imagine. Let's ask God to show us how to use our strengths to make the world a better place and bring glory to Him.

Reflection

Think about the gifts and strengths you have. How can you use them responsibly and in alignment with God's will?

Reflect on the story of Samson and the lessons he learned. How can you apply the lesson of using your gifts responsibly and surrendering to God's will in your own life?

Let's Pray

Dear God, thank You for the story of Samson and the lesson of using our gifts responsibly. Help me to surrender my gifts to You and to use them in ways that honor You and benefit others. Guide me to seek Your will in all that I do. Strengthen me to fulfill the purpose You have for my life. Amen.

27
CALEB'S COURAGE

___ / ___ / _____

> "But because my servant Caleb has a different spirit and follows me wholeheartedly, I will bring him into the land he went to, and his descendants will inherit it."
>
> — NUMBERS 14:24

The story of Caleb is about courage, faith, and trusting God no matter what. Caleb was one of the twelve spies sent by Moses to explore the Promised Land. While ten spies were too scared to believe in God's promise, Caleb and Joshua stood strong. Caleb wasn't afraid to follow God wholeheartedly, even when everyone else doubted.

When the Israelites saw the giants in the Promised Land, they wanted to turn back—but not Caleb! He trusted God's power, knowing that if God made a promise, He would keep it. Caleb's bold faith set him apart, and God rewarded him for it. His story reminds us to trust God, even when life gets tough.

Sometimes, challenges can make you feel like giving up, whether it's school, sports, or friendships. But like Caleb, you can choose to have a "different spirit" and keep believing in God's promises. When we trust Him, He gives us the strength to overcome obstacles. Caleb waited years to see God's promise fulfilled, but he never stopped believing. When we stay faithful, God leads us, strengthens us, and blesses us in ways we never expected!

Reflection

Think about a time when something felt really hard to achieve or when you felt like giving up. How did you handle it?

Did you ask God for help?

Caleb's story shows us that trusting God can help us through anything. How can you trust God more when things feel tough?

Let's Pray

Dear God, thank You for Caleb's example of faith and perseverance. Help me to trust You with all my heart, even when life gets hard. Give me courage to face challenges and strength to keep going. May I always follow You wholeheartedly and believe in Your promises for my life. Amen.

28
JONATHAN'S LOYALTY

___ / ___ / _____

> "Jonathan said to David, 'Go in peace, for we have sworn friendship with each other in the name of the Lord.'"
>
> — 1 SAMUEL 20:42A

The story of Jonathan shows us the power of true friendship and how God works through the people in our lives. Jonathan, the son of King Saul, was a loyal friend to David, even though his father saw David as an enemy. Instead of siding with his father, Jonathan trusted God's plan and remained committed to his friendship with David.

Jonathan's loyalty reminds us that being a good friend isn't always easy. Sometimes, it means standing by someone even when it's hard or unpopular. True friends encourage each other, stick together in tough times, and remind one another to trust God.

JONATHAN'S LOYALTY

Being a friend like Jonathan means more than just having fun—it's about caring for your friends when they need you most. Whether it's offering a kind word, praying for them, or standing up for them, your kindness and loyalty can make a big difference.

Friendship is a special gift from God. When we love and support our friends with faith, we bring joy to others and honor God's plan for our lives. Let's aim to be the kind of friends who reflect God's love and build relationships that last!

Reflection

Think about a friend who has always been there for you. How has their loyalty and kindness made you feel?

What can you do to be a better friend to someone in your life?

Reflect on the story of Jonathan and his faithfulness. How does it inspire you to show kindness and loyalty in your friendships?

Let's Pray

Dear God, thank You for the story of Jonathan and the example of true friendship. Help me to be a loyal and kind friend who supports others, just like Jonathan supported David. Teach me to trust Your plans and to be a light in my friendships, pointing others to You. Amen.

29
JOSHUA'S LEADERSHIP

___ / ___ / _____

"Be strong and courageous. Do not be afraid; do not be discouraged, for the Lord your God will be with you wherever you go."

— JOSHUA 1:9

Joshua's story is a great example of trusting God and being brave. After Moses died, Joshua was chosen to lead the Israelites into the Promised Land. That was a huge responsibility! But God gave him a promise: *"Be strong and courageous. I will be with you wherever you go."* That was all Joshua needed to face his fears and step up as a leader.

We all face moments when life feels tough—starting a new school, facing a big challenge, or trying something new. It's normal to feel nervous, but like Joshua, we can find courage by trusting in God's promises. God is always with us, just like He

JOSHUA'S LEADERSHIP

was with Joshua. When we rely on Him, we can face anything with confidence.

Joshua's courage didn't come from being perfect or knowing everything. It came from trusting that God would guide him every step of the way. Because of his faith, he led the Israelites to victory. His story reminds us that we don't have to let fear hold us back—when we trust God, we can be bold and strong.

When you're in a tough situation, remember that God is with you. He's cheering you on, giving you strength, and helping you succeed. Whether it's standing up to a bully, trying out for a sports team, or tackling a tough school project, you can be brave because God is on your side!

Reflection

Think about a challenge you're facing right now. What makes it feel scary or difficult?

How can you trust God to give you courage?

Take a moment to reflect on Joshua's story. How can his faith inspire you to trust God in your own life?

Let's Pray

Dear God, thank You for the story of Joshua and his amazing courage. Help me to trust Your promises, especially when things feel hard or scary. Give me strength to face challenges and confidence to know that You are always with me. Thank You for guiding me every step of the way. Amen.

30
KING DAVID'S BRAVE HEART

___ / ___ / _____

"The Lord saved me from the lion and the bear. He will save me from this Philistine too!"

— 1 SAMUEL 17:37

David's story is awesome! He was just a young shepherd boy, not a soldier or warrior. But when a giant named Goliath came to fight Israel, David stepped up. Goliath was huge and scary, and everyone else was too afraid to fight him. But David wasn't afraid. Why? Because he trusted God completely.

David had seen God help him before. When lions and bears tried to attack his sheep, God gave David the courage and strength to stop them. He knew God would help him again, even against someone as big as Goliath. So, with just a slingshot and a stone, David went out to fight. He didn't need fancy weapons or armor—he only needed God. And guess what? With one shot, David defeated the giant!

We all have "giants" in our lives. Maybe it's a big test, a tough situation with a friend, or a problem that feels too hard to solve. It's okay to feel nervous or scared, but remember: God is with you, just like He was with David. You don't have to fight your battles alone.

David's courage came from trusting God, not from being the strongest or the smartest. When you face something hard, trust God to help you. He's bigger and stronger than anything you're going through. With Him on your side, you can be brave, no matter what.

Reflection

What is a "giant" you're facing right now?

How can you take a step of faith and trust God like David did?

Think about how God has been faithful in your life before. How can remembering those moments help you face your challenges today?

Let's Pray

Dear God, thank You for the story of David and his brave heart. Help me to trust in Your power, even when I feel scared or unprepared. Remind me of all the ways You've helped me before, and give me the courage to face the challenges ahead. Thank You for being with me every step of the way. Amen.

PART 7

BUILDING HEALTHY HABITS

31
ACTIVE PLAYTIME

___ / ___ / _____

> "Do you not know that your bodies are temples of the Holy Spirit, who is in you, whom you have received from God?"
>
> — 1 CORINTHIANS 6:19A

God gave us amazing bodies, and He wants us to take care of them. One fun way to do that is by staying active and enjoying playtime. When you run, jump, or play, you're not just having fun—you're also keeping your body strong and healthy. It's like saying *"Thank you!"* to God for the gift of your body and honoring Him by taking care of it.

Being active isn't just about staying healthy. It's also a way to bond with friends, learn new skills, and experience the joy of movement. Whether you're kicking a soccer ball, climbing trees, or dancing to your favorite song, these activities help you build confidence and teamwork. God wants us to enjoy life, and being active is a great way to do that!

ACTIVE PLAYTIME

Remember, being active isn't about winning or being the best. It's about trying new things, having fun, and staying positive. Even if you're not the fastest runner or the best jumper, every time you move your body, you're honoring God by taking care of His gift.

As you enjoy your playtime, remember that your body is a temple of the Holy Spirit. Think about how staying active shows gratitude to God and helps you feel happier and stronger. Let your play be a celebration of His goodness!

Reflection

Think about your favorite activities. How do they help you stay active and healthy?

Are you making enough time for active play?

Reflect on the verse from 1 Corinthians 6:19 and think about how taking care of your body honors God. What's one new activity you'd like to try to stay healthy and grow stronger?

Let's Pray

Dear God, thank You for giving me a strong and healthy body. Help me to make time for active play and use my body to honor You. Guide me to choose activities that bring joy, friendship, and growth while taking care of the temple You've given me. May my playtime always bring glory to You. Amen.

32
HEALTHY EATING

___ / ___ / _____

"So whether you eat or drink or whatever you do, do it all for the glory of God."

— 1 CORINTHIANS 10:31

God has blessed us with amazing gifts—our bodies and the vibrant world around us. Healthy eating is a way to honor Him and take care of the temple He has entrusted to us. When we choose nutritious foods like fruits and vegetables or drink plenty of water, we keep our bodies healthy and strong, showing gratitude for His creations.

Imagine your plate filled with different colors, like a beautiful rainbow. Each color represents essential nutrients your body needs to stay healthy. Eating a variety of colorful fruits and vegetables not only nourishes your body but also helps you grow strong, focused, and energized for His work. Similarly, staying hydrated by drinking enough water every day gives your body the refreshment it needs to function properly.

But did you know that your spiritual health is just as important? As water refreshes your body, the living water that Jesus offers refreshes your soul. When we draw closer to Him through prayer and reflection, we are strengthened spiritually. Taking care of our physical and spiritual health allows us to better serve God and others with energy, joy, and purpose.

So, the next time you prepare a meal or pour a glass of water, remember the gift of nourishment God provides. Make your healthy habits a way to thank Him and live for His glory. Let's celebrate the beautiful and nutritious food He has given and drink deeply from His living water that sustains our souls.

Reflection

Think about the colorful foods and drinks you enjoy. Are you making choices that help your body stay healthy?

How does drinking water remind you to refresh your soul with Jesus' living water?

Reflect on 1 Corinthians 10:31 and John 4:14. How can you honor God through your eating and drinking habits?

Let's Pray

Dear God, thank You for providing nutritious food and refreshing water to keep my body strong and healthy. Help me make choices that honor You, both in what I eat and drink. Guide me to take care of the temple You've given me, bringing You glory in all that I do. Amen.

33
CALM BREATHING

___ / ___ / _____

"Be still, and know that I am God."

— PSALM 46:10A

*H*ave you ever felt so worried or overwhelmed that your mind couldn't slow down? Maybe you were nervous about a test, a sports game, or a big change in your life. When life feels like a storm, it's hard to find peace. That's where calm breathing comes in—it's like pressing pause and letting God help you reset.

Take a moment to try it now: Close your eyes, take a deep breath in through your nose, and slowly let it out through your mouth. Do it again, feeling your body relax each time. As you do, imagine God's peace filling your heart, like a warm hug reminding you He's right there with you.

The Bible reminds us in Psalm 46:10 to "be still" and know that God is in control. He doesn't just want us to survive the tough times; He wants us to thrive. When we pause, breathe, and focus on Him, we can feel His presence and comfort, even in the middle of stress.

Calm breathing isn't just about quieting your mind—it's about making space to connect with God. It's like a quick prayer without words, just letting Him know you trust Him. The next time you're feeling anxious or frustrated, remember: One deep breath can be a step toward God's peace. It's your way of saying, *"God, I know You've got this."*

When you practice calm breathing, you'll notice how it helps you handle life's ups and downs. Whether you're facing something big or just need a moment to regroup, God's peace is always just a breath away.

Reflection

Think about a time when you felt anxious or stressed. How did you try to calm yourself? How can calm breathing help you feel closer to God during those moments?

Reflect on Psalm 46:10—how does it encourage you to trust God more?

Let's Pray

Dear God, thank You for the gift of calm breathing and the reminder that I can always come to You for peace. Help me to slow down, take deep breaths, and trust that You are with me in every moment. Teach me to find comfort in Your presence and to feel Your peace, no matter what's going on around me. Amen.

34
TECH BREAKS

___ / ___ / _____

"Do not conform to the pattern of this world, but be transformed by the renewing of your mind."

— ROMANS 12:2A

Why take a tech break? Technology is everywhere—we use screens for homework, games, videos, and chatting with friends. While it's great to have so much at our fingertips, too much screen time can leave us feeling tired, distracted, or disconnected. God didn't design us to live on autopilot with our devices—He made us to experience life fully.

Taking a break from screens helps your mind reset and your body recharge. Instead of scrolling through endless videos, imagine stepping outside to run, kick a ball, or lie in the grass and look at the clouds. Doesn't that sound refreshing? These moments remind us of the beauty God created, the joy of friendships, and the excitement of using our creativity.

TECH BREAKS

This doesn't mean giving up screens forever—it just means making time for other awesome things. Go on an outdoor adventure, try something creative like drawing or building, or hang out with family and friends by playing a game or cooking together. You can also spend time with God by reading your Bible, journaling, or praying in a quiet place.

Each break gives your mind a chance to reset and refresh, just like Romans 12:2a says, *"renewing your mind."* When we step away from screens, we make space to see and experience more of what God has for us!

Reflection

Think about how much time you spend in front of screens. Could you take a short tech break today?

What fun or meaningful things could you do instead?

Reflect on how those moments might bring you closer to God, nature, or the people around you.

Let's Pray

Dear God, thank You for the gift of technology. It helps us learn, have fun, and connect with others. But sometimes, we forget to step away and enjoy the amazing world You've made. Help me to find balance and take breaks from screens so I can refresh my mind and spend time in meaningful activities. Show me how to use technology wisely and enjoy life the way You intended. Amen.

35
SLEEPY TIME ROUTINE

___ / ___ / _____

"In peace I will lie down and sleep, for you alone, Lord, make me dwell in safety."

— PSALM 4:8

Did you know that having a regular bedtime routine can help you wake up feeling refreshed and ready for anything? Sleep isn't just something we do because we're tired; it's a gift from God to help us recharge and stay strong for the adventures ahead.

Think of a bedtime routine as a signal to your body that it's time to relax. Maybe it's reading a cool book about something you love, listening to soft music, or even taking a warm bath. These small habits help prepare your body for rest and create a peaceful environment where you can feel cozy and safe.

Sleep is essential for growing strong, keeping your brain sharp, and staying energized. When you get enough sleep, you'll be better at sports, have more fun with friends, and feel ready to tackle schoolwork. Think about it like this: a well-rested you is the best version of you!

Make it a habit to go to bed at a specific time each night and do calming activities before you sleep. Create a space that feels comfortable, like a blanket fort where you can relax and feel safe. As you lie down, remember that God is watching over you, protecting you, and helping you find peace.

Reflection

What's your current bedtime routine?

Could you add something to make it more relaxing, like talking to God, journaling your thoughts, or even stretching?

Think about Psalm 4:8 and how it reminds you that God's care helps you feel safe and rested.

Let's Pray

Dear God, thank You for the gift of sleep and the chance to rest my body and mind. Help me create a bedtime routine that helps me feel calm and ready for rest. Remind me that You are always watching over me, keeping me safe through the night. May I wake up refreshed and ready to face the new day with energy and joy. Amen.

PART 8

ANIMALS IN THE BIBLE

36
THE PATIENT TURTLE

___ / ___ / _____

> *"But those who wait on the Lord shall renew their strength; They shall mount up with wings like eagles, They shall run and not be weary, They shall walk and not faint."*
>
> — ISAIAH 40:31 (NKJV)

Have you ever watched a turtle slowly make its way to its destination? Turtles teach us something amazing—patience. They move one step at a time, never rushing, but always moving forward. Even though their journey might be slow, they always reach their goal.

In life, we often want things to happen quickly, whether it's learning something new, fixing a problem, or waiting for a special moment. But patience, like the turtle shows us, is powerful. It's not always easy to wait or trust that things will work out, but God promises that when we trust Him and wait on His timing, He will give us the strength we need.

THE PATIENT TURTLE

Isaiah 40:31 reminds us that those who wait on the Lord will renew their strength. Like the turtle keeps going without giving up, God helps us keep moving forward, even when the journey feels long or tough. He knows the bigger picture and will guide us at the perfect time.

Patience takes practice. Each time you trust God instead of rushing—whether it's being kind to a sibling, working on a long project, or praying for an answer—you're building faith. Think of God as your coach, cheering you on as you patiently run the race of life. Every small step matters, and when you trust Him, you'll find you're stronger than you realized. So, take a lesson from the turtle—steady, patient, and always moving forward with faith in God's plan.

Reflection

Can you think of a time when you felt frustrated because you had to wait? How did it feel, and how could trusting God have helped you?

What's one area in your life where you need to practice more patience?

Let's Pray

Dear God, thank You for teaching me the importance of patience through the turtle's example. Help me to trust Your perfect timing, even when it feels hard to wait. Give me strength to keep going when the journey feels long. Thank You for always guiding me and helping me grow in faith. Amen.

37
THE CRAFTY SNAKE

___ / ___ / _____

"Be alert and of sober mind. Your enemy the devil prowls around like a roaring lion looking for someone to devour."

— 1 PETER 5:8

Have you heard about the snake in the Garden of Eden? This story teaches us the importance of staying alert and making wise choices. When Adam and Eve encountered the crafty serpent, they were tricked into disobeying God. The serpent deceived them into eating from the one tree God told them to avoid, leading to serious consequences. This reminds us how important it is to be discerning and to base our decisions on God's truth.

In life, we often face situations that seem tempting or harmless at first. But not everything is as it appears. Just like Adam and Eve, we may hear voices trying to pull us away from what is right. These could come in the form of bad influences, dishonest choices, or even doubts about God's Word. That's why we need to rely on God's truth—it guides us in the right direction, even when we feel uncertain.

Being alert doesn't just mean watching out for obvious danger; it means staying close to God so we can recognize deception when it comes. Through prayer, reading the Bible, and listening to trusted mentors, we grow in wisdom and learn to make choices that honor Him.

The next time you face a tough decision, take a moment to pause and seek God's guidance. His truth will never lead you astray. When we trust Him and follow His commands, we experience the blessings that come from walking in obedience!

Reflection

Think about a time when you had to make a decision between what was easy and what was right. How did you handle it?

How does God's Word help you make wise choices in your daily life?

Let's Pray

Dear God, thank You for showing us the importance of making wise choices. Help me to be alert and stay focused on Your truth. Protect me from anything that could lead me astray, and guide me to always follow Your Word. Thank You for being my source of wisdom and light. Amen.

38
THE FAITHFUL DOG

___ / ___ / _____

"So Jesus answered and said to her, 'O woman, great is your faith! Let it be to you as you desire.' And her daughter was healed from that very hour."

— MATTHEW 15:28 (NKJV)

Did you know that a dog is mentioned in one of Jesus' stories? A Canaanite woman came to Jesus, pleading for her daughter's healing. Even when others tried to discourage her, she didn't give up. She believed in Jesus' power and trusted that He could help her. Because of her strong faith, Jesus praised her and healed her daughter immediately.

The comparison to a dog in this story teaches us something special. Dogs are loyal, trusting, and persistent—they never give up on those they love. The woman's faith was just like that. She knew Jesus was her only hope and refused to let go of her belief in Him.

THE FAITHFUL DOG

Faith isn't just about trusting God when things are easy. It's about holding onto Him even when life feels uncertain. This story shows that faith isn't about being perfect—it's about believing in Jesus' love and power, no matter what.

God wants us to come to Him with boldness and trust. Just as He cared for the Canaanite woman and her daughter, He cares for us too. Let's strive to be like the faithful dog in this story—loyal, persistent, and full of trust in the One who never lets us down.

Reflection

Think about a time when you needed something so deeply that you refused to give up. How did it feel to rely on someone else's help?

Reflect on the Canaanite woman's unwavering faith in Jesus. How does her story challenge you to trust God fully?

What are some things you can bring to God in faith today?

Let's Pray

Dear God, thank You for showing me the power of strong faith. Help me to trust You, even when life is hard. Teach me to be loyal and persistent in my faith, knowing that You care for me deeply. Amen.

39
THE TALKING DONKEY

___ / ___ / _____

"Trust in the Lord with all your heart, and lean not on your own understanding."

— PROVERBS 3:5 (NKJV)

Have you ever heard of Balaam's talking donkey? It's one of the most surprising moments in the Bible! Balaam was on a journey when his donkey suddenly stopped in the road. Balaam didn't know it, but an angel of the Lord was blocking their path. The donkey could see the angel and was trying to protect Balaam. Frustrated, Balaam struck the donkey—until God opened the donkey's mouth, and it spoke! The donkey explained its actions, and in that moment, Balaam's eyes were opened to see the angel too.

This story teaches us an important lesson: God can use anything or anyone to guide us. Sometimes we think we know the best path, but God sees what we can't. Just as Balaam's donkey recognized danger, God often places signs in our lives to help us make wise choices. When we rely only on our own understanding, we might miss His guidance. But when we trust Him, He leads us toward safety and blessings.

God may not send a talking donkey to guide us, but He does speak to us in different ways—through His Word, prayer, our circumstances, and wise people around us. When we listen and trust Him, we can navigate life's challenges with confidence, knowing He is always watching out for us.

Whenever you face a tough decision, remember Balaam's story. Trust that God sees what you can't and lean on His wisdom instead of your own. He promises to guide us when we put our faith in Him!

Reflection

Think about a time when you didn't know what decision to make. Did you pause to ask for God's guidance?

What are some ways you can listen to God's voice in your daily life?

Let's Pray

Dear God, thank You for always guiding me, even when I don't understand. Help me trust You with all my heart and listen carefully to Your voice. Teach me to rely on Your wisdom, not my own. Protect me from danger, and lead me on the right path. Amen.

40
THE DILIGENT ANT

___ / ___ / _____

"Go to the ant, you sluggard! Consider her ways and be wise."

— PROVERBS 6:6 (NKJV)

*H*ave you ever watched ants as they work? These tiny creatures may seem small, but they are incredibly diligent, hardworking, and organized. The Bible encourages us to learn from them! Ants gather food in the summer to prepare for the winter, showing us the importance of planning ahead and working hard for the future. Their example reminds us that success doesn't come from laziness, but from consistent effort and preparation.

Diligence is a trait we can all practice in daily life. Whether it's studying for a test, practicing a new skill, or helping at home, putting in effort now leads to rewards later. Hard work isn't always easy or fun, but it helps us grow and accomplish great things. When we stay faithful with our responsibilities, we honor God by making the most of the opportunities He gives us.

Like the ants, we should use our time and talents wisely. Instead of putting things off or getting distracted, we can commit to working with focus and perseverance, trusting that our efforts will lead to good results. God calls us to be responsible, to work hard, and to glorify Him in everything we do.

Let's take inspiration from the ants and put our faith into action. When we approach life with diligence and responsibility, we prepare for the future and honor God. Let your hard work be a reflection of your gratitude for the gifts and opportunities He has given you!

Reflection

What is one task or goal you've been avoiding? How can you approach it with diligence like the ants?

Reflect on Proverbs 6:6. How does it inspire you to work hard and plan for the future while trusting God with the results?

Let's Pray

Dear God, thank You for the example of the ants and their diligence. Help me stay focused, work hard, and use my time wisely. Give me the strength to overcome laziness and see the value of preparation. Guide me to use my abilities for Your purpose. Amen.

PART 9

DISCOVERING GOD'S CREATION

41
THE BEAUTY OF CREATION

___ / ___ / _____

> *"The heavens declare the glory of God; the skies proclaim the work of his hands."*
>
> — PSALM 19:1

Have you ever stopped to admire the beauty around you? From towering mountains to tiny butterflies, from colorful flowers to rushing waterfalls, nature is filled with God's amazing design. Psalm 19:1 says, *"The heavens declare the glory of God; the skies proclaim the work of his hands."* Every part of creation reflects His power, wisdom, and creativity.

When we look at the vast sky or the details of a blooming flower, we see the care of our Creator. Everything in nature has a purpose, from the smallest insect to the tallest tree. God designed it all with precision, showing that He values both beauty and purpose in His creation.

Appreciating nature also reminds us to take care of it. God has given us the earth as a gift, and it's our responsibility to protect it. Whether it's recycling, caring for animals, or planting trees, our actions can reflect gratitude for what He has entrusted to us.

The wonders of creation not only reveal God's greatness but also remind us of His love. The same God who made the stars and the oceans also created you with care and purpose. Let the beauty of the world inspire you to praise Him and live with gratitude for all He has made!

Reflection

Think about a natural scene or creature that has captured your attention. How does it make you feel?

How does it remind you of God's creativity?

Reflect on the verse from Psalm 19:1. How does it inspire you to appreciate and care for God's creation?

Let's Pray

Dear God, thank You for the beauty of Your creation. The wonders of nature reflect Your glory and wisdom. Help me to appreciate and care for the world You have made. Give me the understanding to be a good steward of the environment and to reflect Your creativity in all that I do. May I always find joy in the beauty of Your creation. Amen.

42
GOD'S MASTERPIECE

___ / ___ / _____

"I praise you because I am fearfully and wonderfully made; your works are wonderful, I know that full well."

— PSALM 139:14

Hey there! You're not just an ordinary kid. Nope! God made you one-of-a-kind. He didn't copy and paste when He created you. Instead, He gave you your own special talents, abilities, and personality. Think about it—your laugh, your ideas, even the way you see the world—all of that was designed by God! Pretty cool, huh?

When you hear the word "masterpiece," you might think of famous paintings or awesome sculptures. But did you know YOU are one of God's masterpieces? Yep! God made you with care and love, like an artist working on their favorite project. Every part of you was planned on purpose. Your talents, your personality, even the things that make you different—they're all part of God's perfect design.

Sometimes, you might feel like you're not good enough or that you don't fit in. But guess what? You don't have to be like anyone else. Your worth doesn't come from what you do or what people think of you. It comes from the fact that God made you special. And that's something no one can take away!

God didn't make you to hide who you are. He made you to shine! Maybe you're good at sports, drawing, making people laugh, or helping others. Whatever your gift is, use it! When you share your talents, encourage a friend, or just be yourself, you're showing the world how awesome God's creation is.

Reflection

Take a moment to think about what makes you special. What talents or abilities has God given you?

How can you use them to bring joy to others and honor God?

Remember, Psalm 139:14 reminds us that you are fearfully and wonderfully made. How does knowing this inspire you to see yourself in a new way?

Let's Pray

Dear God, thank You for making me fearfully and wonderfully. Help me remember that I'm Your masterpiece and to love the unique person You made me to be. Show me how to use my talents to bring happiness to others and honor You. Amen.

43
CARING FOR CREATION

___ / ___ / _____

"The earth is the Lord's, and everything in it, the world, and all who live in it."

— PSALM 24:1

*D*id you know that we have a responsibility to take care of the environment?

Caring for creation means knowing the value and beauty of the world around us. It's about doing small but important things to protect and take care of our planet. This might include picking up trash, recycling, saving water, or being careful about how much electricity we use. It's all about making choices that show we respect what God has made.

God gave us this amazing world to live in, filled with trees, animals, rivers, and mountains. But He also asked us to be good stewards—that means caretakers—of His creation. When we take care of the environment, we're showing respect and gratitude for the gifts God has given us.

When we care for the earth, we honor God's design. It's like saying thank you to Him for giving us such a beautiful place to live. Plus, taking care of creation isn't just about us—it's about making sure future generations can enjoy it too. Imagine if we all worked together to keep the oceans clean, the forests healthy, and the air fresh. How awesome would that be?

Even small actions, like turning off the lights when you leave a room or planting a tree, can make a big difference. God sees those efforts and loves it when we take care of His world.

Reflection

Think about one practical step you can take to care for the environment. How does it align with your responsibility as a steward of God's creation?

Reflect on the verse from Psalm 24:1. How does it inspire you to be mindful of the world and its resources?

Let's Pray

Dear God, thank You for entrusting us with the care of Your creation. Help us to be mindful of our responsibility as stewards of the environment. Guide us in making choices that protect and preserve the world You have made. Give us wisdom to take practical steps to care for the earth and show gratitude for Your gifts. Amen.

44
THE MIRACLE OF LIFE

___ / ___ / _____

"For you created my inmost being; you knit me together in my mother's womb."

— PSALM 139:13

Have you ever marveled at the wonders of birth, growth, and the cycle of life? From the sprouting of a seed to the birth of a baby, these moments are filled with awe and beauty.

Every life is a precious gift from God. He is the Creator of life, and each person, plant, and animal is intricately designed and formed by His loving hands. We are fearfully and wonderfully made, with unique qualities and purposes.

When we reflect on the miracle of life, we develop a deep appreciation for the value and sanctity of every living thing. We recognize the interconnectedness of all living beings and the responsibility we have to protect and nurture life in all its forms.

THE MIRACLE OF LIFE

Let us cherish and celebrate the gift of life. Whether it's a tiny seed sprouting or a new baby entering the world, these moments remind us of God's faithfulness and His ongoing work of creation. May we treat all life with respect, care, and love.

Reflection

Think about a moment in nature or a memory of a new life you have witnessed. How does it remind you of God's creative power and the preciousness of life?

Reflect on the verse from Psalm 139:13. How does it inspire you to appreciate the miracle of life?

Let's Pray

Dear God, thank You for the miracle of life and the beauty that surrounds us. Help us to appreciate and cherish every living thing, recognizing Your hand in creation. Give us hearts that value and respect life in all its forms. May we nurture and protect the gift of life as a reflection of Your love. Amen.

45
FINDING GOD IN NATURE

___ / ___ / _____

"The heavens declare the glory of God; the skies proclaim the work of his hands."

— PSALM 19:1

Have you ever felt a sense of peace and wonder when you spend time in nature?

Nature is like a grand display of God's creativity and power. The vibrant colors of flowers, the majestic mountains, and the gentle rustling of leaves all point to the glory of our Creator. When we take time to observe and appreciate the natural world, we can find moments of awe and inspiration that draw us closer to God.

Spending time in nature provides us with opportunities for reflection and prayer. It is a place where we can quiet our minds, listen to the sounds of creation, and seek God's presence. Whether it's a walk in the woods, watching a sunset, or stargazing at night, these moments allow us to connect with our Creator and experience His peace.

So, let's make it a habit to spend time in nature, appreciating its beauty and seeking moments of reflection and prayer. Whether alone or with others, let's open our hearts to the wonder of God's creation and let it lead us to a deeper connection with Him.

Reflection

Think about a favorite spot in nature that brings you joy and peace. How does it help you feel closer to God?

Reflect on the verse from Psalm 19:1. How does it inspire you to seek God's presence through observing nature?

Let's Pray

Dear God, thank You for the beauty of nature and the moments of peace and wonder it brings. Help me to connect with You as I observe Your creation. Open my eyes to Your presence in the natural world. Guide me to find moments of reflection and prayer that deepen my relationship with You. Amen.

PART 10

KINGS OF THE BIBLE

46
THE WISDOM OF KING SOLOMON

___ / ___ / _____

> *"For the Lord gives wisdom; from His mouth come knowledge and understanding."*
>
> — PROVERBS 2:6

Have you heard of King Solomon and his incredible wisdom? The Bible tells us that true wisdom comes from God.

Solomon was one of the wisest people to ever live, but here's the coolest part—when he became king, he didn't ask God for riches or fame. Instead, he asked for wisdom to lead his people. He wanted to make the best choices and knew he needed God's help to do it.

God was so pleased with Solomon's request that He gave him wisdom, along with wealth and honor. Solomon became famous for making wise decisions that helped others. His story teaches us that when we seek wisdom from God, He will provide what we need to make good choices.

But what is wisdom? It's not just knowing a lot of facts or being smart. Wisdom is using what you know to make choices that honor God and help others. It's about knowing right from wrong and choosing what's right—even when it's hard.

If you ever feel stuck or unsure, don't worry. You can pray and ask God for wisdom, just like Solomon did. You can also read the Bible and talk to people you trust, like your parents or teachers. God loves to help us make decisions that bring us closer to Him and bless those around us!

Reflection

Think about a time when you didn't know what to do. How can you ask God for wisdom in moments like that?

Reflect on Proverbs 2:6 and remember that wisdom comes from God. What's one way you can use God's wisdom to make a good choice this week?

Let's Pray

Dear God, thank You for the story of King Solomon and how he trusted You to give him wisdom. Help me to seek Your wisdom when I face decisions, big or small. Teach me to make choices that honor You and help others. Thank You for always guiding me and giving me the understanding I need. Amen.

47
KING JOSIAH'S FAITHFULNESS

___ / ___ / _____

"I have chosen the way of faithfulness; I have set my heart on Your laws."

— PSALM 119:30

*H*ave you heard of King Josiah and his commitment to following God's commands?

Josiah became king when he was just eight years old—can you imagine that? Even though he was young, he wanted to do what was right in God's eyes. As he grew older, Josiah discovered the Book of the Law and realized that the people weren't following God's commands. He didn't ignore it or pretend it wasn't a big deal. Instead, Josiah took action. He got rid of all the idols in the land and made sure that people were worshiping the one true God.

King Josiah teaches us what it means to stay faithful to God, even when it's not easy. He didn't just follow God's commands because he had to. He did it because he loved God and wanted to live a life that honored Him. That's what faithfulness is all about—choosing to follow God's ways, no matter what, and trusting that His plans are always best.

Faithfulness isn't just about rules. It's about loving God so much that you want to live your life His way. It's like choosing to eat healthy because you know it's good for you, even if candy seems more fun at the moment. God's laws help us live in a way that brings us closer to Him and fills our lives with good things.

Reflection

Think about a choice you've made recently. Was it the kind of choice that honors God?

How can you show faithfulness to God in the way you talk, act, and treat others? Reflect on Psalm 119:30 and consider how you can set your heart on following God's ways this week.

Let's Pray

Dear God, thank You for the story of King Josiah and how he stayed faithful to You. Help me to choose faithfulness every day by following Your commands and living the way You want me to. Teach me to love Your laws and trust that Your ways are best. Thank You for always being with me and guiding me. Amen.

48
KING SAUL'S OBEDIENCE

___ / ___ / _____

"But Samuel replied: 'Does the Lord delight in burnt offerings and sacrifices as much as in obeying the Lord? To obey is better than sacrifice, and to heed is better than the fat of rams.'"

— 1 SAMUEL 15:22

Have you heard of King Saul and his struggles with obedience? The Bible tells us that God values obedience more than outward acts of worship.

Saul had a big job as Israel's first king, but he didn't always make the best choices. One time, God gave him a clear command, but Saul decided to do things his own way. He thought offering a big sacrifice would make up for disobeying God's instructions—but it didn't. His story teaches us how important it is to listen to God and follow His guidance, even when we don't fully understand why.

KING SAUL'S OBEDIENCE

Obedience to God isn't just about following rules—it's about showing love and trust. When we obey God, we're saying, *"I trust that You know what's best for me."* And the good news? God's commands are always meant to help us, not make life harder.

Sometimes, obedience can be tough. Maybe you've wanted to ignore what your parents told you because you preferred your own way, or you've been tempted to follow the crowd instead of doing what's right. In those moments, remember Saul's story: obeying God is always better than trying to do things on our own.

Reflection

Can you think of a time when you had to choose between doing what you wanted and doing what was right?

How can you trust God and obey Him, even when it's hard?

Reflect on 1 Samuel 15:22 and how it reminds us that obedience is more important than outward acts of worship.

Let's Pray

Dear God, thank You for teaching me the importance of obedience through King Saul's story. Help me trust You and follow Your instructions, even when I don't fully understand. Give me a humble heart that listens to Your voice and chooses Your way over my own. Amen.

49
THE LEADERSHIP OF KING CYRUS

___ / ___ / _____

> "The King will reply, 'Truly I tell you, whatever you did for one of the least of these brothers and sisters of mine, you did for me.'"
>
> — MATTHEW 25:40

Have you heard of King Cyrus and his remarkable leadership? The Bible tells us that he played a key role in rebuilding the temple and restoring God's people.

King Cyrus was a powerful ruler, but what made him special was how he used his power—not just for himself, but to help others. Instead of focusing only on his own kingdom, he helped God's people rebuild their lives and their faith. His story teaches us that true leadership isn't about being in charge—it's about making a positive difference.

Cyrus understood that his power and influence were gifts from God, and he used them to bless others. His actions remind us that when we help those in need, we are also serving God. That's what real leadership looks like!

You may not be a king (yet!), but you have your own kind of influence—at school, at home, or with friends. Leadership isn't about being the loudest or strongest; it's about making choices that help others feel seen, loved, and supported.

Look around—who needs encouragement or kindness? Maybe a new student at school, a sibling having a rough day, or a friend who needs support. When you choose to care, you're showing the same kind of servant leadership that King Cyrus did.

Reflection

Take a minute to think: How can you use your gifts—your kindness, your skills, your time—to make a difference for someone?

Remember Matthew 25:40. How can you serve someone else as if you're serving God? It could be as simple as a smile, a kind word, or standing up for what's right.

Let's Pray

Dear God, thank You for King Cyrus and his example of leadership. Help me see ways to make a difference, no matter how small. Teach me to be kind, thoughtful, and brave enough to lead by serving others. Amen.

50
THE PERSEVERANCE OF KING ASA

___ / ___ / _____

"The Lord is my strength and my shield; my heart trusts in Him, and He helps me. My heart leaps for joy, and with my song I praise Him."

— PSALM 28:7

Have you heard of King Asa and his unwavering trust in God?

King Asa's story is an awesome example of what it looks like to lean on God when life gets tough. He wasn't perfect, and he didn't have all the answers, but he knew where to turn for help —straight to God! Whether it was an army attacking his kingdom or big decisions he needed to make, Asa didn't let fear stop him. Instead, he trusted God to give him the strength to push through.

Here's the cool part: Asa didn't rely on his own strength or ideas. He prayed, stayed faithful, and waited for God to guide him. And you know what? God showed up for him every time.

THE PERSEVERANCE OF KING ASA

His story reminds us that God is our shield when life feels overwhelming. No matter what challenges you're facing, God is strong enough to help you through it.

Perseverance means sticking with something even when it's hard. It's about trusting God to help you keep going, even when you feel like giving up. Maybe it's a tricky math problem at school, a tough situation with friends, or a sport you feel like quitting. Remember, God is right there with you. When you rely on His strength, amazing things can happen!

Reflection

What's one challenge you're facing right now?

How can you rely on God's strength to help you keep going?

Think about Psalm 28:7 and how it can encourage you to trust God even when things are tough. How can you use this truth to find joy in the middle of your challenge?

Let's Pray

Dear God, thank You for the example of King Asa and how he stayed strong by trusting in You. Help me to rely on Your strength when I feel weak or overwhelmed. Give me the courage to keep going, even when things get tough, and remind me to praise You in all situations. Thank You for being my shield and my help. Amen.

PART 11

DEVELOPING RESILIENCE

51
THE RACE OF FAITH

___ / ___ / _____

"Let us run with perseverance the race marked out for us."

— HEBREWS 12:1B

Have you ever thought about life being like a race? The Bible compares our faith journey to a long-distance run—one that takes perseverance and determination.

In a race, runners train hard and push through challenges to reach the finish line. The same is true for our faith. There will be moments of doubt, temptation, or discouragement when we feel like giving up. But God is always there, cheering us on and giving us the strength to keep going. He has a special path for each of us, and our job is to stay on it, no matter how tough it gets.

Running the race of faith means keeping our eyes on Jesus, the ultimate example of perseverance. He faced hardships but never gave up. When we look to Him, we find the strength to overcome obstacles. Trusting God is like having a great coach—He knows exactly what we need to succeed. He picks us up when we stumble and encourages us when we're tired.

This race isn't about being the fastest or strongest—it's about finishing well. Living a life that pleases God, staying faithful, and growing closer to Him makes us stronger with every step.

Reflection

Think about something in your life right now that feels like a hurdle or a steep hill. Maybe it's a tough subject at school, a disagreement with a friend, or feeling like you don't measure up. How can you lean on God to help you keep going?

Remember, He's running alongside you, cheering for you every step of the way. The verse from Hebrews 12:1b reminds us that perseverance is key. What can you do today to stay on track and keep running your race?

Let's Pray

Dear God, thank You for being with me in life's race. When things feel tough, help me to keep going and trust in Your strength. Remind me that I'm not running alone—you are guiding me, encouraging me, and giving me the perseverance I need. Keep me focused on You so I can grow stronger in my faith every day. Amen.

52

BUILDING A STRONG FOUNDATION

___ / ___ / _____

> *"Therefore everyone who hears these words of mine and puts them into practice is like a wise man who built his house on the rock."*
>
> — MATTHEW 7:24

The parable of the wise builder teaches us an important lesson: having a strong foundation matters. Imagine a house—if its base is weak, it won't stand when storms come. But if it's built on solid ground, it can handle anything. Our lives work the same way. When we build on God's truth, we stay strong no matter what challenges come our way.

A strong foundation doesn't happen overnight. It's built by hearing God's words and actually living them out. That means choosing kindness over anger, honesty over lies, and trusting God even when things don't go our way. It also means staying faithful to God's plan, even when we don't fully understand it.

Every time we choose to follow Him, we grow stronger in our faith.

Life will have storms—moments when you feel left out, struggle in school, or face tough decisions. But when you build your life on God's truth, those storms won't knock you down. His Word gives you the courage and wisdom to stand firm no matter what happens.

It's like a superhero—they don't get their powers all at once. They train, learn, and face challenges to grow stronger. Every time you show kindness, forgiveness, or patience, you're like a wise builder, laying another brick on your foundation of faith!

Reflection

Is there an area in your life where you need to feel stronger? Maybe it's trusting God more or making better choices.

How can His words help you stand firm? Matthew 7:24 reminds us that building our lives on God's truth is the best choice we can make.

Let's Pray

Dear God, thank You for teaching me about the wise builder. I want my life to be strong and steady, built on Your truth. Help me to listen to Your words and live them out every day. Give me the strength to make good choices, even when it's hard. Thank You for being my solid rock. Amen.

53
PETER - FROM FAILURE TO SUCCESS

___ / ___ / _____

> "But he said to me, 'My grace is sufficient for you, for my power is made perfect in weakness.' Therefore I will boast all the more gladly about my weaknesses, so that Christ's power may rest on me."
>
> — 2 CORINTHIANS 12:9

*P*eter's story is an awesome reminder that failure isn't the end—it's often just the beginning of something greater. Peter, one of Jesus' closest friends, messed up big time when he denied knowing Jesus. But instead of staying down, Peter experienced God's amazing grace and forgiveness. This failure didn't define him; instead, it helped him grow stronger in his faith. He learned to rely on God's power and found strength even in his weaknesses.

God's grace is like a safety net that catches us when we fall. When we admit that we need His help and trust Him with our weaknesses, He can do incredible things in and through us. Failure doesn't mean you're finished—it's a chance to learn, grow, and let God show you just how powerful He is.

Peter didn't let his mistakes keep him down. Instead, he came back stronger, full of humility and faith. He became a bold leader, spreading Jesus' message to others. His weakness turned into an opportunity for God to work through him, and the same can happen in your life. Your failures are not the end of your story—they're stepping stones to something greater when you let God take control.

When you make a mistake, it's easy to feel like giving up or believing you're not good enough. But remember, God's grace is bigger than any failure. Just like Peter, you can bounce back stronger. Mistakes are a chance to learn and grow, not a reason to quit. Ask for God's forgiveness and trust Him to help you get back on track. Through His grace, your weaknesses can become a way for His strength to shine in your life.

Reflection

Take a moment to think about a time when you felt like you failed or weren't strong enough. What did you learn from that experience?

How can you trust God's grace to help you move forward? Let the verse from 2 Corinthians 12:9 remind you that His power is made perfect in your weakness.

Let's Pray

BIBLICAL TEACHINGS

Dear God, thank You for Peter's story and how You turned his failure into success. Help me to learn from my mistakes and trust in Your grace. Teach me to rely on Your strength in my weaknesses, knowing that You can use them for good. Thank You for loving me even when I mess up. May Your power shine through my life, and may I bring glory to Your name. Amen.

54
OVERCOMING CHALLENGES AT SCHOOL

___ / ___ / _____

"I can do all this through him who gives me strength."

— PHILIPPIANS 4:13

Have you ever heard stories about students who faced tough academic challenges but didn't let those challenges stop them? Maybe they struggled with a tricky subject or had a ton of homework but kept working hard until they succeeded. Those stories are powerful because they show what perseverance, dedication, and faith can do.

Sometimes, school feels overwhelming. Maybe it's a math problem that doesn't make sense, a project that feels impossible, or even the pressure of trying to do your best every day. It's easy to feel like giving up. But the good news is, you don't have to face these challenges alone. God is with you, ready to give you the strength to keep going.

When you lean on God, He gives you the power to tackle even the hardest tasks. With His help, you can face academic challenges with courage and determination. It's not just about working hard—it's about trusting that God will guide you and give you the strength you need. The verse from Philippians reminds us that we don't have to do everything on our own. God's strength fills in where ours runs out.

Each challenge is an opportunity to grow. You're not just learning new things at school—you're also learning how to persevere, to stay focused, and to trust God more. These lessons will stay with you long after the school year is over. When you succeed, it's not just because of your hard work but also because of God's presence and power in your life.

Reflection

Think about something at school that feels tough for you right now. Maybe it's a subject you don't understand or a goal that feels out of reach. How can you approach it with perseverance and faith?

Let the verse from Philippians 4:13 remind you that God's strength is always with you. What steps can you take today to rely on Him and move forward?

Let's Pray

Dear God, thank You for being with me in every challenge I face at school. Help me to trust in Your strength and work hard, even when things feel tough. Give me the courage to keep trying and the wisdom to know that You're always there to help me succeed. Thank You for helping me grow in knowledge, perseverance, and faith. Amen.

55
SPORTSMANSHIP AND PERSEVERANCE

___ / ___ / _____

"I press on toward the goal to win the prize for which God has called me heavenward in Christ Jesus."

— PHILIPPIANS 3:14

Have you ever watched an athlete face challenges, setbacks, or even failure, only to get back up and keep trying? Their determination to improve and achieve their goals is so inspiring. Athletes remind us of the importance of sportsmanship and perseverance—two qualities that don't just matter in sports but also in life.

Athletes often have to work through difficulties like losing a game, missing a goal, or struggling with a tough opponent. But instead of giving up, they keep practicing and pushing themselves. That kind of perseverance takes hard work, discipline, and a positive attitude. They remind us that setbacks are not the end of the story—they're just a part of the journey.

In our own lives, we might not be playing in a big game, but we still face challenges and setbacks. Whether it's failing a test, not making the team, or dealing with something difficult, it's easy to feel discouraged. But just like athletes, we can press on toward our goals. When we focus on learning from our mistakes and growing stronger, we develop perseverance, which helps us face life's challenges with courage.

The verse from Philippians encourages us to keep our eyes on the ultimate goal—living a life that honors God and trusting Him to guide us toward His promises. God is cheering you on, reminding you that your efforts are not in vain. Every time you choose to keep going, you're becoming stronger and building character that will help you in all areas of your life.

Reflection

Think about a goal or challenge you're facing right now. How can you keep pressing forward, even when things get tough?

Let the verse from Philippians 3:14 inspire you to keep your eyes on God and trust Him to help you reach your goals.

Let's Pray

Dear God, thank You for the example of perseverance and sportsmanship in athletes. Help me to press on toward my goals with determination, even when I face setbacks or failures. Teach me to trust in Your strength and to never give up, knowing that You are always guiding me. Thank You for being with me on this journey and helping me grow stronger in my faith and my life. Amen.

PART 12

PLANNING FOR THE FUTURE

56
DREAM BIG

___ / ___ / _____

> *"For I know the plans I have for you," declares the LORD, "plans to prosper you and not to harm you, plans to give you hope and a future."*
>
> — JEREMIAH 29:11

Have you ever imagined what your future might look like? Maybe you've thought about becoming a firefighter, an inventor, a teacher, or even an astronaut. God has placed unique dreams and aspirations in your heart for a reason. Those dreams are part of the amazing plans He has for you.

Dreaming is a special gift from God. It allows us to picture the possibilities and potential He's given us. When you dream big, you're opening your heart to God's guidance and trusting Him with your future. You're saying, *"God, I believe You have incredible things planned for my life."*

The verse from Jeremiah reminds us that God's plans are always good. He wants you to grow, succeed, and have a future filled with hope. When you align your dreams with God's purpose for your life, amazing things can happen. It's like teaming up with the best coach ever—someone who knows exactly what you need to achieve your goals and reach your full potential.

Reflection

What's a dream or aspiration you have for your future?

How does it fit with God's plans for your life?

Reflect on the verse from Jeremiah 29:11 and let it inspire you to dream big, knowing that God's guidance and love are always with you.

Let's Pray

Dear God, thank You for placing dreams and aspirations in my heart. Help me to dream big and trust that Your plans for my life are good. Guide me as I pursue my goals, and give me the wisdom to align them with Your purpose. Thank You for always being with me and for helping me believe in a hopeful and exciting future. Amen.

57
GOAL-SETTING 101

___ / ___ / _____

"Commit to the LORD whatever you do, and he will establish your plans."

— PROVERBS 16:3

Setting goals helps us turn our dreams into actionable steps. One helpful method is using SMART goals. Let's break it down:

S - Specific: Make your goal clear and specific. Define exactly what you want to achieve.

M - Measurable: Set a way to measure your progress. It could be through milestones or specific metrics.

A - Achievable: Make sure your goal is attainable. Consider your abilities, resources, and the time you have.

R - Relevant: Your goal should be relevant to your dreams and aspirations. It should align with your values and priorities.

T - Time-bound: Set a deadline for achieving your goal. Having a timeframe creates a sense of urgency and helps you stay focused.

When we commit our goals to the Lord, seeking His guidance and wisdom, He establishes our plans. He can help us align our goals with His purpose and give us the strength and resources we need to achieve them.

So, let's set SMART goals that reflect our dreams. Write them down, make them specific, measurable, achievable, relevant, and time-bound. And most importantly, commit them to the Lord, trusting Him to guide us every step of the way.

Reflection

Think about a dream you have and break it down into a SMART goal. How does this goal align with your dream?

Reflect on the verse from Proverbs 16:3. How does it inspire you to commit your goals to the Lord?

Let's Pray

Dear God, thank You for the gift of setting goals. Help me to set SMART goals that align with my dreams and aspirations. Guide me as I commit my goals to You. Give me the wisdom, perseverance, and resources I need to achieve them. May my goals reflect Your purpose for my life. Amen.

58
LEARNING FROM ROLE MODELS

___ / ___ / _____

"Follow my example, as I follow the example of Christ."

— 1 CORINTHIANS 11:1

We can gain valuable insights and inspiration by looking at the lives of successful individuals who have achieved their goals.

Role models are like real-life superheroes. They show us how to set goals, work hard, and keep going even when things get tough. Whether it's someone famous, a teacher, a coach, or even your own parents, their stories remind us that anything is possible when we stay focused and trust in God.

Think about someone you look up to. Maybe they're great at something you love, like sports, art, or science. How did they get there? It didn't happen overnight! They probably had to face challenges and work really hard to reach their goals. That's what makes them inspiring—they didn't quit, even when it was hard.

The coolest thing about role models is that they show us what's possible for our own lives. When you see someone who started just like you and achieved something amazing, it's like a reminder: *"Hey, you can do this too!"* Learning from them can give you the confidence and direction you need to chase your own dreams.

But the best role model of all is Jesus. He shows us how to live wisely, stay strong, and trust God. When you follow His example, you learn to be kind, brave, and full of faith, no matter what comes your way.

Reflection

Think about a role model or someone you admire who has achieved their goals. What can you learn from their experiences?

Reflect on the verse from 1 Corinthians 11:1. How does it inspire you to follow their example and the example of Christ?

Let's Pray

Dear God, thank You for the role models in my life who inspire me to achieve my goals. Help me to learn from their experiences and apply the lessons they teach. Guide me in following their example as I follow the example of Christ. Give me the wisdom and perseverance to work hard towards my dreams. In Your name, I pray. Amen.

59
BUILDING SKILLS AND KNOWLEDGE

___ / ___ / _____

"The heart of the discerning acquires knowledge, for the ears of the wise seek it out."

— PROVERBS 18:15

Take time to reflect on your goals and consider the specific skills and knowledge required to reach them. Ask yourself, "What do I need to learn? What skills do I need to develop?"

It's important to know what you need to learn and work on to reach your goals. Whether it's practicing math, improving in sports, or learning how to play an instrument, taking action helps you grow. Don't wait for skills to magically appear—get started and keep going!

There are so many ways to build your skills and knowledge. You can read books, take classes, ask for help from a mentor, or practice hands-on. Each step you take adds to your abilities and brings you closer to achieving your goals.

Remember, building skills isn't just about becoming good at something—it's also about using what you learn to help others. God wants you to grow and use your talents to make a difference. When you work on your skills with His guidance, you'll not only reach your goals but also inspire and help the people around you.

Reflection

Think about a goal you have and the skills or knowledge you need to develop to achieve it. How can you acquire the necessary skills and knowledge?

Reflect on the verse from Proverbs 18:15. How does it inspire you to seek knowledge and develop your skills?

Let's Pray

Dear God, thank You for the opportunities to learn and grow. Help me to identify the skills and knowledge I need to reach my goals. Guide me in seeking out learning opportunities and developing my abilities. Grant me wisdom and discernment as I acquire knowledge. May I use my skills and knowledge to make a positive impact in the world. In Your name, I pray. Amen.

60
ADAPTING AND ADJUSTING

___ / ___ / _____

"Many are the plans in a person's heart, but it is the LORD's purpose that prevails."

— PROVERBS 19:21

While it's essential to set goals and make plans, it's equally important to recognize that life is full of surprises and unexpected turns. Being willing to adapt and adjust your plans allows you to respond to new opportunities and challenges that come your way.

Sometimes, things don't go the way we expect, and that's okay! Maybe your plans need a little tweaking, or you find a better way to achieve your goals. Adjusting doesn't mean you're failing—it means you're learning and growing. God can use these changes to lead you to something even better.

Being flexible is a superpower. It helps you face setbacks without giving up. When you adapt, you open yourself up to new ideas, skills, and possibilities that you might not have thought of before. It's all part of the journey God has planned for you.

Remember, even when your plans change, God's purpose for your life remains constant. Trust that He's in control and guiding you every step of the way. When you embrace change and rely on Him, you'll find strength and confidence to keep moving forward.

Reflection

Think about a time when you had to adapt or adjust your plans due to unforeseen circumstances. How did it impact your journey toward your goals?

Reflect on the verse from Proverbs 19:21. How does it inspire you to trust in God's purpose and be open to adjusting your plans?

Let's Pray

Dear God, thank You for the reminder to be flexible and adaptable in my plans. Help me to trust in Your purpose and guidance as I make adjustments along the way. Grant me the wisdom to know when to change my course and the courage to embrace new opportunities. Keep my ultimate goals in sight and help me stay focused on them, even as I navigate unexpected changes. May Your purposes prevail in my life. In Your name, I pray. Amen.

THE END?

Hey, you made it to the end—how cool is that? Seriously, give yourself a high five (or maybe a fist bump). I'm so glad you spent some time with this book, and I hope it gave you some awesome ideas and helped you grow in your faith. If you thought this was cool, I'd love to hear what you think!

Here's the deal: if this book helped you out, made you think differently, or even just gave you something to talk about, ask your parents or guardian if you can leave a quick review. It's super easy! Just scan the QR code below and you're good to go. Or, if you're on Amazon, search for this book, scroll down to the review section, and hit *"Write a customer review."* Boom—you've just shared your thoughts with the world. How awesome is that?

THE END?

SCAN ME

But before you go, let me tell you something important: your story isn't over—it's just getting started. Every day is like a blank page, and you get to decide what goes on it. You've got so much potential to be strong, kind, and full of faith. Even when life gets tricky (and yeah, it will sometimes), remember that God's got an amazing plan for you. Keep going, keep growing, and keep being the awesome person you are.

Oh, and don't forget this: you don't have to have it all figured out right now. God works with what you've got—even the messy, imperfect stuff—and He can do some pretty epic things through you. So take what you've learned, share it with your friends, and keep building a solid foundation of faith. You're not in this alone—God's got your back, always.

Stay awesome, keep crushing it, and remember—you're made for big things!

P.S. If you're hungry for more, I've got other books on Amazon under Biblical Teachings. Check them out when you're ready for the next adventure!

www.ingramcontent.com/pod-product-compliance
Lightning Source LLC
Chambersburg PA
CBHW052048070526
44584CB00017B/2095